All Within You

The Beginning

notionpress
.com

All Within You

The Beginning

MAHALAXMI NAIDU

notionpress.com

Notion Press

Old No. 38, New No. 6

McNichols Road, Chetpet

Chennai - 600 031

First Published by Notion Press 2015

ISBN 978-93-5206-448-9

Dedicated to

My dearest,

Amma, Appa

&

Renu

Rest in Peace

Miss you all...

"What a piece of work is man!
How noble in reason!
How infinite in faculty, in form and moving!
How express and admirable!
In action, how like an angel!
In apprehension, how like a god!
The beauty of the world, the paragon of animals!"

By Shakespeare

Contents

GOD IS GREAT

MOTIVATIONAL AND INSPIRATIONAL

LIFE

DREAM

LOVE

MOTHER

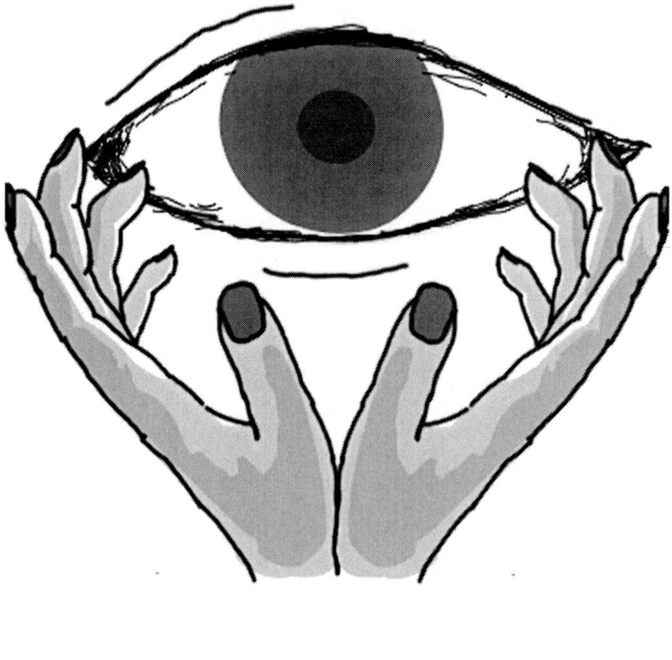

GOD IS GREAT

Somebody is watching over you,
with their wide eyes.

There...your ever brightest
and beautiful future lies!

I know you are there!

I know you are there…
for the hearts which are wounded,
for the souls which are abandoned,
for the minds which are threatened,
for the eyes without vision.

I know you are there…
to eradicate the darkness,
to alleviate the agonizing pain,
to wipe down throbbing tears,
to eliminate life's all fears.

I know you are there…
to show the ray of hope,
to the suffering wrecked souls.
to give the desired comfort,
for those alone…

I know you are there.

Just in two words I state my feelings,
Thank you Lord for everything!

Profound within

Thank you Lord

When I am down and cheerless, when I feel terribly unhappy,
When I feel lonely, when I feel sad & sometimes gloomy,
I am so glad to know that you are always there for me.

When the days simply seems to go wrong & sometimes off beam,
When I keep failing & see success very far, & tears end up to be a stream,
I am so glad to know that you are always there beside me.

When life looks no more beautiful, when music sounds awful,
When friends becomes foe, to make the life more dreadful,
I am so glad to know that you are always there to hear me.

When "love" loses its charm, when "care" loses its meaning,
When sadness becomes life & not ready to free me,
I am so glad to know that you are always there to bear me.

When folks blame me, torment me for doing nothing wrong,
When they try to degrade, disgrace & demean me,
I am so glad to know that you are always there to stand for me.
When I, no more can withstand & when am livid with life's plan,
When I just seem to stumble, stagger, plunge & fall,
I am so glad to know that you are always there to hold me.

When I struggle, strive & strain to get the work full done,
For which only horrid spiteful remark is what I get in return,
I am so glad to know that you are always there within me.

I thank you from the core of my heart & soul,
for being with me, always, profound within me.
For the unconditional selfless love,
that you keep bestowing upon me,
For the life you gave me & for all your support,
For the hope you give me each day, that life is not that dire.
And for everything which you have given to me,
I am thankful to you My Dearest Lord.

THANK YOU…

Collation of these two godly words,
whole world's beauty it holds

Thank You. . .Lord

Thank you God for blessing us with love & affection,

Thank you for all things you have bestowed upon us.

Thank you Lord, for the smiles and happiness you have given,

Thank you for the life which is as bright as a burly and vivacious sun.

Thank you My Lord for everything.

Thank you.

When humanity crosses its boundaries,
human domain gets affected,
so you, so I!

From God to the World

You let me down, disappointed I am,
All over the world,
blood is shed.
My heart cries out of pain,
losing my spirit too,
Helpless I am, left with no further clue,
My children, with pride I created you,
to adore the life to its fullest.
I wanted you all to be happy,
But this creation has become my regret.
Situation all over is worse.
Nothing left to endorse.
I am disappointed and distraught.

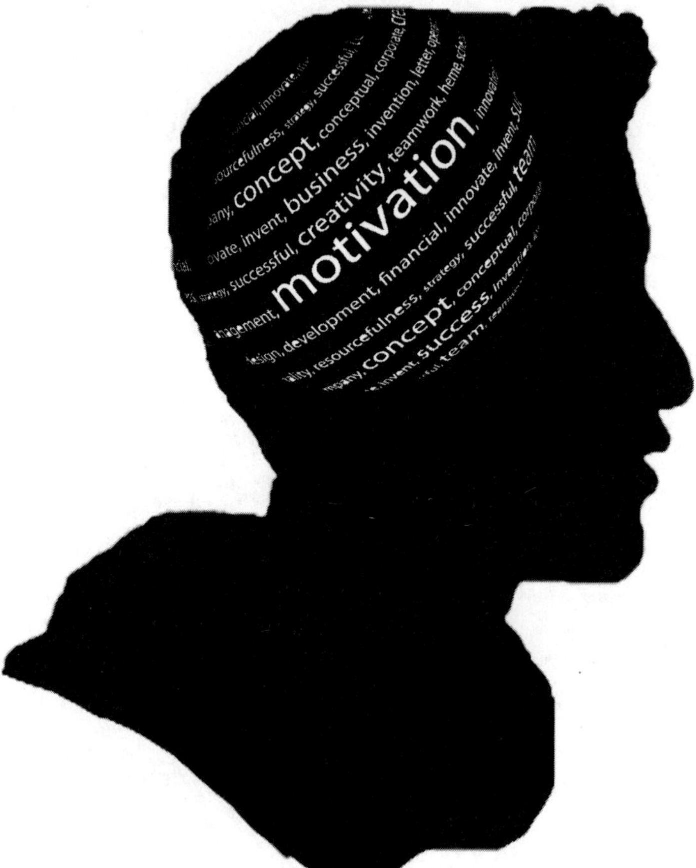
motivation
concept, conceptual, corporate
invent, business, invention, letter
successful, creativity, teamwork
management
design, development, financial, innovate, invent
resourcefulness, strategy, successful, team
concept, conceptual
success, invention
team

MOTIVATIONAL AND INSPIRATIONAL

Whole of the cosmos

is within us.

Allow self, to discover it.

All Within You

Within you lies the strength, to fight battle that's
extreme,
Within you lies the courage to accomplish your unfulfilled
dreams.

Within you lies the acumen, to accomplish your goal in
life,
Within you lies the providence, to have your share of
fortune in rife.

Within you lies the zeal, to encounter romance,
Within you lies the artistic move, desirable to dance.

Within you lies the faith, to believe in Miracle,
Within you lies the purity, looked-for to admire the nature.

Within you lies the passion, to discover your occurrence,
Within you lies the obsession, to revere your essence.

Within you lies the curiosity, to unravel the mystery of Universe,
Within you lies the adequacy, to endorse this enigmatic world.

Within you lies the peace, to comprehend the silence of sea,
Within you lies the radiance, to eradicate night's obscurity.

Within you lies the guts', to accept challenges coming your way,
Within you lies the happiness, to relish each moment of the day.

Life… a merry go round.

Or perhaps, an icy track leading to our covet.

Or a velvety avenue full of preeminent opportunities,

…giving shapes to all our naïve desires.

Life's ride

Flow like river and shine like sun,
Believe in you, believe that you can.
Swim like fish and run like horse,
Try your best, let your soul endorse.
Smile like a child, yes… the innocent one,
And compel all the obstacles with speed to run.
Set a goal to reach, and have determination,
It's wonderful to have in life a worthy mission.

Stand like a rock, in matters of principle,
Attitude, that matters, for the leader to rule.
Dance like a peacock, even in no rain,
And let the universe take care of your pain.
Bloom like a flower, to spread out fragrance,
Let the world be aware of your significance.
Sing like a nightingale in a melodious way,
And enjoy the incredible ride in life's sway.

Formation of a new art, new world, new life….
is an outcome, of our prevailing Imagination.

Imagination Rules the World!

Imagination rules the world, this was once quoted,
Having it in originality is for what, we are motivated.
It can take you to the wildest part of the world's corner,
to ocean, top of the mountain, it can take you anywhere.
Can refresh you, your mind & soul,
Isn't it a fact that imagination rules the world?

We can be in the sea or under the tree, or in the place of greenery,
We can be anywhere, any place, wherever we want to be.
We can walk on the fire, or on the prickly pieces of glasses,
With a smile on face, having no sign of grievances.
We can reach on the top of a mountain hill with a jump one,

We can swim like a fish and like a horse we can run.
Wonder, in a day, a new born to become an adult,
With no diplomacy, we can talk whatever we felt.
Life with no pain, no tears, no sorrow and grief,
Imagine a life filled with laughter, joy & relief.
Having health, wealth & power throughout the life,
Everywhere in the world, all to have it in rife.
Imagine a distinct creativity of creation,
Ought to be a magnificent piece of imagination.

Imagine a night with shining sun around,
And with joy, the moon dancing down.
Imagination is fun & can actually revive your mind,
To imagine rather unique, one of it's kind.
Such a wonderful gift to human, God has bestowed,
Beyond doubt, imagination… truly rules the world.

Life's rule is pretty simple,

You struggle... you gain!

Quit not... the birdie says

With the rise of the sun, I rise
I wonder...ahead what lies!
Before nightfall could end my day
I have precious one whole day

Oh man, wake up!
Sleep not... when your goal is halfway
Oh man, wake up!
Hear me; see what a birdie wants to say

We have nothing but few moments to live
Tomorrow is unknown and furtive
Life is beautiful, live fullest each day
Be thankful, in every little way

Oh man, listen!
Life is short and concise
Oh man, listen!
Love and live life

Failing, falling must not stop you
Failure is a part, it must not haunt you
Dream big and achieve your goal
Universe exists within you, don't ignore.

Oh man, go on!
Quit not....on your dreams.
Oh man, go on!
Miracles do happen in extremes.

Live beautifully,
Experience divinity.

Act

Your act shall be an act, to admire and adore,
In this whole world, by each and every soul.
Shall not only in words, but also in deeds,
Have desires to reach the acme, which lies there above.
To twinkle like a star, to shine like a sun,
To do everything right, to be the best one.
To dance in the rhythm of pouring rain,
Without concerning happiness or pain.
Don't you stop, even if you fall,
Go on, till you attend your "final" call.
Your act shall be an act, to admire and adore,
In this whole world, by each and every soul.

LIFE

Thoughts…

the soul reason.

for the good, bad and ugly!

Thoughts

You think differently,
definitely not like me.
I think differently,
unlike you, certainly.
Why not revere thoughts of each other,
which is inimitable and beyond doubt not similar.
Your thoughts are full of purity and harmony,
It's clearly of life on earth to be as same as heaven above.
My thoughts are more matter-of-fact,
I rummage around for the ways to improve the world.
Don't mix-up with my words, not an attempt to disdain
your thoughts,
just trying to apprise you, with your own thoughts.

Very often we think all, is so very beautiful,
but fail to get into the depth and ensure the root.
There's lot to be changed in this world,
Humans are killing humans in the name of caste and
community,

This destroys the nation's oneness and integrity.
None setting example, none exist to lead.
Blocked are minds, blocked are ways,
Wealth & Power, a driving craze.
Let's combine thoughts of yours and mine,
precious is life, let us remind.
Let's be humane, a message to humankind.
Live in peace and let live,
in this, we shall believe
Let's spread peace and love,
all over the world, also be known..
nothing here, belongs to anyone!
With pro-tem arrival and,
Impromptu departure,
It's time to comprehend,
None belongs to any one,
No one owns this world!

I said,

…am ready to carnage self, to be you,
Isn't it worth living even for a day… being you!

O' Bird, Can I be YOU?

O' Bird!,
Wish I could be you,
I would fly, the way you do,
no boundaries, no stopping,
no consent, no commands to follow,
no nasty thoughts, no mean people to deal with,
I will be me, with no societal pressure,

O' Bird, can I be you?
I want to fly high in the amazing sky
with widened wings and broadened vision
just to fly high…extremely high
no one to curb, with no limitation.

O' Bird!
I would love to be you,
Can I escape from here too?
Humans kill each other here,
in the name of caste and creed,
some do it for wealth and power,
painfully, a matter of greed,

O' Bird, can I be you?
I want to fly high in the amazing sky,
with widened wings and broadened vision,
just to fly high…extremely high,
no one to curb, with no limitation.

O' Bird!

Unpredictable is life, the famous, once said,
let me take you little further….

Unpredictable Life...

Life is unpredictable, they said.
Never did I believe this as true.
How can life be good...
...and same time cruel too?

How unpredictable life can be...
I realized...
When,
A woman, being childless for many years,
Living, but with no reasons to live.
When she finally conceived,
Heavenly her world perceived,
Couple desired to happily live,
Gave birth to a beautiful child,
But during labour, she had to die!

How unpredictable life can be...
I realized...
When,
This man had whole world's wealth,
Loving family, vibrant life and health,
Fearless was he, had a secured future,
But milliseconds of earth tremor,
Quaked the earth, quaked his life too,
In nature's cruel blow,
he lost everything in one go!

How unpredictable life can be!
I realized….
When,
A poorest of a poor man,
Struggled to get through each day,
No dreams, no desires or vision,
Except for a full tummy and no hunger fray,
Casually given free lottery,
Makes him a millionaire one day,
Everything is thrown onto him,
Beyond his wildest dream!

How unpredictable life can be!
I realized…
When,
We strive hard each day,
For a secured tomorrow,
We allow the moments to fleet,
Vaguely, with worry and fear,
We keep thinking of our future,
When we don't even know,
if today's sunset we will witness,
May be… this very moment turns out
…to be our last breath!

How unpredictable life can be
I realized…
When,
Life turns up and down,
Beyond what we could ever envision!

Dreams never scream, in the…
scary and lonely nights,
They are not afraid of darkness,
they don't require lights!

Step into my dream

Step into my dream, and see the world through eyes of mine,
Let's create a world, where everything is well and extremely fine.

Come with me, let me take you somewhere,
Somewhere, some place where life is fair.

Somewhere,
the sky meets the earth.
Somewhere,
Life is full of mirth.

Somewhere,
Rainbow appears throughout the year.
Somewhere,
Everything is upright and sheer.

Somewhere,
There's no misery and dearth.
Somewhere,
There's no spite, a kind of filth.

Somewhere,
There's no darkness around.
Somewhere,
Only beam can be found.
Somewhere,
There's laughter all that we could hear.
Somewhere,
There's no terror and no sign of fear.

Somewhere,
There's no suffering and pain.
Somewhere,
There's nothing as loss and gain.

Somewhere,
the stars talk to us.
Somewhere,
Life - no less than a fest.

Somewhere......some place...
Step into my dream and see the world through eyes of mine,
This is my world, where everything is well and extremely fine.

Jealousy leads to Evil thinking,
Evil thinking leads to destruction.
For others, the ruin is transitory,
but, your disaster will be for eternal.
So why feel jealous?

Jealousy. . .a Killer

Outrageously jealous was he,
Couldn't bear their…
happiness,
wanted to see them in…
a ruinous mess!

Desperately, wanted to steal smiles…
from their smiling faces,
couldn't bear to see them winning….
life's races,

Their enhanced life meddled with…
his inner peace,
While their eyes wept,
his heart happily beeped,

Restless was he, in his life throughout,
neither was he in peace, nor in bliss.
His life was lost in vain,
In the end, he found himself in a vicious drain.

Of late, he realized,
Jealousy stirs and drills within,
besides it kills within!

Arrogance,
for what…?

be happy and humble,
life is extremely short!

Hello, Arrogant people!

I care a damn…
of what you think of me,
and what or who I am!

I am better than you,
for what you are…
As a human

Do not disregard,
Or belittle the lowly me,
My essence cannot be slayed
Be wary of me.

Your wealth, power and pride,
Nothing does it holds.
Nothing belongs to anyone,
No one owns the world.

The greatest of great is,
only one there above,
Just to him, the whole…
World on knee bows!

They boasted in pride,
for having travelled worldwide,
have they even heard of
"Eden's Garden - a Paradise"!

In search of Paradise

A bud of night stepped into my dream and showed
me a ray of hope.

Hope took me to touch the essence & spirit of my
determined goal.

Goal on triumph, allowed me to cherish the ecstasy of
victory.

Victory on other hand, pampered me with abundance of
royalty in life.

Life with hope, goal and victory took me to the farthest
place....

...a place which looked like a paradise.

A bud of night stepped into my dream and showed me a
ray of hope,

Hope took me to the world of resilience and fortitude.

Fortitude with will power helped me gain the ultimate desired supremacy,

Supremacy, full of power, allowed me to be a sovereign in life.

Life with Hope, Fortitude and Supremacy took me to the farthest place,

….a place which was no less than a paradise.

A bud of night stepped into my dream and showed me a ray of hope.

Hope showed me the way going towards faithfulness and devotion.

Devotion enhanced my soul by giving eternal peace.

Peace gave me serenity of a sea, enlightening my soul and life.

Life with Hope, devotion, peace took me to the farthest place.

….a place…truly a paradise.

Troubled with life, a downhearted father,
screamed at his 10 year old son,
for wasting time on roving near the crawling ants.

After a long pause,
his son asked, unpretentiously,
"Father, are ants, spiders Gods Miracles?",
"There is nothing as Miracle", angry father grumbled

To which, the son replied
"Ants tells us to work hard & save for the rainy day,
Spiders taught the greatest king to never give up"
..this is what my teachers say.,
Are they wrong?"

Instead of answering his son's questions,
he thanked his son for giving an answer.
Miracles come in any form.

Marvelous Miracle

Rainbow a miracle
And miracle is the rain
Tears a miracle
Sign of happiness and pain

Moon a miracle,
And miracle is the sun
Love… a miracle
Life gives to everyone

Flower a miracle
And miracle is its fragrance
Heart a miracle
And miracle is its significance

To adore almighty
I have every reason
I have every reason to thank him
for the marvels of miracle
…the marvelous miracle

Life a miracle
And miracle is its existence
Mirror a miracle
And miracle is the reflection

Fire a miracle
And Miracle is the spark
Day a miracle
And miracle is the dark

World a miracle
And miracle is the formation
God a miracle
And miracle is his creation

To adore almighty
I have every reason
I have every reason to thank him
for the marvels of miracle
...the marvelous miracle

Caterpillar or Butterfly,
All is One, In the End.
In conflict, since ages, I wonder why!

Panorama of Life

Childhood says:
Eat, sleep, play, be merry, is my life's purpose,
live merrily with no tension and no strain,
get my things done, by alluring each one,
am contended always, each day is like a fest,
I think, I am the best of all the rest.

Teenage says:
"I know everything"; can change the world even,
Distinctive, can do all that I want. Me – "a style icon",
a sovereign I am, not depended on anyone,
I am full of dream, can fulfill it with all my guts,
I think I am the best, of all the rest.

Middle age says:
Much matured and I've capacity to understand,
life not just a past time, I do comprehend,
believe in hard work and determination,
will reach my goal with zeal and zest,
I think I am the best of all the rest.

Old age says:
Full blown, a part of conclusion,
valued for my advice and virtuous suggestions,
can unwind any time, don't disregard… I am a veteran,
a gold ingot, passed through all kind of life's test,
I think I am the best, of all the rest.

All-is-one, In-the-End.
Entails to comprehend!

Education is vast, like the widened sky that's blue,
Vision of it, shall be supreme and broadened too.

Bachelor of Arts. . .So What?

So what,
If I am a student of Arts.
What makes you to,
degrade me?

With Science,
You become a Doctor,
Or Scientist.

With Commerce,
You become a Number Genie,
Or a Mathematician.

But with Arts,
You become a HUMAN!

Don't we desperately need…
more of these…
to mend this pugnacious world.
Your thoughts please!

With great brainteasers,
greatest mysteries are solved!

Provoked Brain!

Not all Intelligent are Successful,
Are all Successful, Intelligent?

Not all Modest are Respected,
Are all Respected, Modest?

Not all Loving are Loved,
Are all loved ones, loving?

Not all Creative are Artist,
Are all Artist, Creative?

Not all Philosophers are Thinkers,
Are all Thinkers, Philosophers?

Not all Famous are Virtuous,
Are all Virtuous, Famous?

Think about it!

Extremely beautiful,
and amazing is life,

Need help?
since you think otherwise!

Oh. . . Negative people!

Why is the sun round, not square?
Shape of moon is also indecorous

Erroneous is the contour of twinkling star,
Can't understand, why it has to be so far?

The darkness of night is illogical,
The brightness of the day is laudable.

The birds clamor is so very grating
The dancing trees are not fascinating.

A rainy day is so very muddy,
Same as a finicky crying baby,

Nature around is so imperfect,
All is wrong, all incorrect

They see all flaws; it makes them feel dreary,
Beware…they are our negative folks, always gloomy!

Luck, What you are?

a miracle…

a wonder…

a dream…

a jinx…

Stroke of Luck

When I try, try & try, put my heart & soul to have the task fulfilled,
enormous obstacles gear up to stub on me, brings me to a standstill,
I wonder, if this is what is known to be the stroke of luck.

I worked hard & hard, every moment & hour, of my entire life,
I envy my colleague for having been promoted, I guess for hardly working,
I wonder, if this is what is known to be the stroke of luck.

Each penny I saved to own a small house in this town, it's still a dream for me which is yet to be accomplished,
my so called friendly & spend thrift neighbor, believed never in saving, just invited me for a royal dinner, as 1 million dollar has won by him,
I wonder, if this is what is known to be the stroke of luck.

I loved someone truly, gifted so many things, and proposed as well, for which I was told "I will think & tell",
That somebody is now married to the one, who looks sloppier than me & is too older,
I wonder, if this is what is known to be the stroke of luck.
Oh dear luck, if you can hear me, please come and pop in my life as well,
embrace & bestow your kindness upon me,
Just want to meet "the wonderful you - stroke of luck".

Future is bright,
If you think right!

Foresee

Among famous names,
your name will appear one day,
Among famous faces,
Recognized, will be your face one day.

We search our fate in hands and stars,
What we have within, we ignore them at all.
Believe that you are a unique person,
Explore your talent in this wonderful world.

It's your choice, you can make it or break it,
why cry, go ahead and grab it,
Life gives chance to each and every one,
It's on you, what you choose from.

Believe one day fortune will be chasing you.
That day fortunate day, is on the way to greet you.
Be prepared for that opportunity.
To become, one day a legendary.
That day fortunate day is on its way to meet you.

DREAM

Dreams rotted within you,
is a forgotten chapter,
and forgotten you!

Now is the Time…

Dreams, dreams my dearest dreams,
Now is the time to come true,
How long will you…
be concealed in my head?
It's time to arise
and move forward.

Dreams, dreams, oh dreams!
Be not so hazy,
Instead, become a reality.
Would you be contented…
to remain just an illusion?
Don't you want to live
and show the world your essence?
Nothing will you gain,
by being an endearing fantasy.
Now is the time to emerge,
become a reality

Dreams, dreams my dearest dreams,
Now is the time to come true.
How long will you…
be concealed in my head?
It's time to arise,
and move forward

Dare…dare…dare!
Dreams are the hopes, life gives you,
Believe in it. It does come true!

Dare to Dream

Dare to dream of flying high,
Dream of touching moon in the sky.
Dream of victory, dream of luxury,
Dream that your life is filled with glory.

Dare to dream of exquisite skies forever,
Dream that we are a worthy endeavor.
Dream the wildest dreams, so you can see,
Dreaming is more than a fantasy.
Dare to dream of being a Pinnacle,
Dream of Life, a blow of raffle.
Dream of wealth, dream of fame,
Dream of everything, there's no one to blame.

Dream of you, through your eyes,
Dream though, it may not be much of a surprise.
That while you dream enjoying the view,
Do wish your dream one day to come true!

LOVE

Those fearless,
end up falling in love!

Fray in Love

Waves of life tells me to tell you what is felt by my heart,
My mind tells heart to think before expressing my feelings,
Feelings are mine....that's for you,
In this battle of heart and mind,
Petrified I....
What if I lose you?

Love disappears,
gives no clue,
but, let it not leave behind
a “dead” you!

Lost Love

I never realized, but how could I?
Unbelievable that our love has died.

You said,
I mean the world to you,
that you will love me forever...
this is what you intended to do

You said,
you will be eternally mine,
and, I mean everything to you.

But everything seemed to be a forbidding lie,
Alas! Our love has painfully died.
I wonder why?
I wonder why!

Love… true or fake,

an eye is enough, to recognize.

Love is in the air...

My Love for you is true, very true,
Deep within my heart, it's you, only you,
Listen to my heart's beat, what it wants to say,
Just snoop the rhythm, rhythm of this loving day.
The day when I saw you, am being called an alien,
My friends think, to you, I have lost everything.
Bewildered I am, tell me what to do,
Just want to be in love, in love with you.

I am learning to enjoy the pour of rain,
Each drop is easing my heart's endearing pain.
Birds, trees, flowers looks new to me,
Wasn't I sloppy? to contempt all these.
I feel to be, on top of this world,
Each moment is so magnificent to adore.
So much, a love can bestow upon me & you,
Love is amazing, isn't a terrific thing to do?

Your smile is so precious, a treasure of mine
I am blessed, to cherish with it for a lifetime.
Blissful to know that your heart beats only for me,
And each beat takes my name, thinking of me.
Believe, in me, that's all I want from you, my love,
I will make you my life, my destiny and my world.
From the core of my heart, I care for you,
I am blessed as I am in love...in love with you!

Love is that petite spark,
enough to lighten up…
a darkest realm.

Wonderful Love

Each moment of this day has euphoria in it, elation of
which makes my existence worthwhile.
Each touch of yours, with affection and caring words
makes me realize,
With love, the world looks so beautiful, like a heaven in
disguise.

When you look at me, tons of virtuous emission passes
through your vision, touching core of my soul.
When you look at me, your sparkling eyes gives me hope
to live each day with warmth and love.
Love is indeed wonderful, beyond doubt; it changes us &
our world.

When you hold my hand, you make me feel I have the
backing of the whole universe,
When you hold my hand, I feel the whole world is worth
living, as it looks truthful and candid.
Love is great, the best gift of God to Human, with love
every day is eternal,
and at its best.

Fate brought us together,

It is our choice whether to…

continue or end!

I Swear

I Swear,

I will be your one true love,
only you, I will adore.
I will care for you always,
I will not leave you in anyways.

I Swear,

I will not affront you any time,
I will be your life's sunshine.
I will be your victorious destiny,
I will be an escort in life's journey.

I Swear,

I will make you my heart and soul,
only you, I will revere & adore.
For you, I will sacrifice everything,
without you, this world means nothing.

I Swear,

You are my fate & fortune,
you are my star, sun and moon.
You are my love, my desire,
except you, nothing I wish more.

I Swear,

I will be your friend just the best,
I will be with you in life's trial & test.
I love you from the core of my heart,
from you, I will never be apart.

I Swear,

I will be yours forever & ever,
Will I hurt you - no, never.
My endless love is only for you,
all my ways reaches only to you.

I Swear,

No clue what is stored in our fate,
but, will love you until my last breath.
I love you…just believe in me,
I live in you & you live within me….

I Swear…

Countless stars in the dark sky,
awaits eagerly to have a glimpse of my love.
And my love, unknown of this fact,
on trivial matters, frowns!

If you...

If you want to be somewhere, my dear,
then be in my life forever and ever.

If you want to care for someone, my dear,
then let that be me, just hold me near.

If you have something, to give me, my dear,
then give me your heart, to treasure it forever.

If you want to take, something from me, my dear,
then take control on my life, for now & for ever.

If you have a dream to fulfill in your life,
Let that dream be, of me, becoming your wife,

If you have a space in your world somewhere,
Let me stay all my life with you there.

If you think someone loves you more than me,
It has to be my soul, loving you selflessly.

If I ever had to leave you & depart the world,
I will still be there next to you being a loving soul.

My love for you is growing by each passing day.
I just love you for what you are in every way.
If you ever think, I am not made for you
Then allow me to depart the world.

If you think I will then stop loving you,
Let me tell you, I will love you even more.

Love knows no boundaries,
Love needs no consent,
It's an emotion,
so divine, so pure.

In Love

The cloud of happiness shrieks mutely in its rhythmic tone,
Each drop from ocean chuckles in a cadenced manner to let all know,

The twinkling stars in the sky flickers blissfully today,
Each leaf of trees applauds gleefully today, revealing the truth,

The zephyr embraces me ceaselessly with endorsement,
Each wave of stream bops with joy telling the world of marine,

That….I am in love with you!

My wait for you will be worthwhile,
Only if the time agrees to standstill!

Be with me…

Each step – A Mêlée,
Victory will be mine,
If with me, is you.

I will over power,
pits of each fray…
with me, if there's you.

Glare in the dark,
Hope in the spark,
I see only…with you!

Life's journey....
a beautiful poem,
with you.

With you

With you, I feel,
I am in the seventh heaven & in the cloud nine,

With you, I feel,
I am cheerful, content and always fine,

With you, I feel,
life is beautiful, full of shine,

With you, I feel,
the world & universe is for me & mine.

With you, I feel,
I have everything I wanted to have one day,

With you, I feel,
I have every reason to be glad in every way.

With you, I feel,
I am secured, loved and adored always.

With you, I feel,
I am cared, admired and accepted every little way.

With you, I feel,
I can own the world if I ever wanted to.

With you, I feel,
I can do what I ever wanted to,

With you, I feel,
I am respected for what I am and all that I do.

With you, I feel,
I am here in the world exclusively for you.

With you, I feel,
I am your valuable treasure.

With you, I feel,
I hold a bright and a beautiful future.

With you,
I feel, all my dreams are turning true,

With you, I feel,
my life was nothing without you.

Thank you for being there for me.

MOTHER

If a return be granted ever,
I will bring you back and treasure forever!

Come Back to Me…

Very often, my heart cries for you, wants you to be in the vicinity of my heart,
Very often, I think of the verdict of God, his motive of taking you away,
I had only you, as a friend, as a guide, as a teacher, whom I can trust anytime any day.
Then why on earth, I am left alone without you; I dreadfully wanted you, for me, to stay,
I needed you beside me, to hold me, to support me, to embrace me,
My dear mother, please come to me, come back to me.

Loneliness has become my comrade, memories - my brainwave, prayer - my breath,
Every moment I convince myself that you don't subsist any more in this world,
My tears doesn't stop from falling, my heart doesn't stop from moaning,
I wanted you throughout my life, you are my life's intact yearning,
You were my valor. Privileged & Secured, your presence would make me,
My dear mother, please come to me, come back to me.

Rest in Peace, my mother dear,
with no pain….no fear.

I will keep you in my heart,
and in remembrance….

You are now in the heavenly land,
in God's caring hands.

Have peaceful sleep,
Rest in peace.

Miss You

Although death has taken you away very far from me,
Dear mother, you will always be there in my heart, soul & empathy.
My heart still pines for you, my eyes are still wet, yearning for you,
Oh mother dear…every day, every moment a lot I miss you…..

You were my friend, a sturdy support & a guide in disguise,
So dim was I to hurt u at times in the rim of dice.
I want you back in my life eternally, Oh dear.
That's my gloomy hearts unfulfilled desire.

Wonder, Oh lord, if given a chance to turn back time,
And have my divine mother everlastingly in my life once again,
miss you mom

NATURE

Nature, is that gift of God,
which the humankind...
has trounced it many times,
...in many ways,
And yet it smiles back, selflessly!

Beauty of Nature

Exquisiteness of the sky cannot be expressed in any words,
Lovely twinkling uncountable diamonds, all it holds.
Every leaf of a tree and every drop from an ocean,
Enlightens us with the nature, that's so magnificent.

Each wave tells us not to lose hope in life,
Take on what is thrown on you, even in rife,
Choice is yours, you may take it or snub it,
But be known that something great is hidden in it.

The sun, the moon and the stars above,
Conveys so many things to the world.
Each playing their role efficiently,
Reminding us to perform our duties well.

Nature's beauty in itself is the marvel of almighty,
It has been made for us, to cherish,
Let's adore it and respect it by heart
Let's confess - it is our lives' important part.

Let rhythm, touch our soul…

once in a while!

In search of Rhythm

Rhythm… is it in the dripping rain?
Or when we shriek out of pain.

Rhythm… is it in the evening breeze?
Or in the dancing trees.

Rhythm…is it life - a sign of existence?
Or a sign of persistence.

Rhythm… is it in a girl's talk?
Or in a peacock's walk.

Rhythm…is it in the lightening & thunder?
Or when children laugh in wonder.

Rhythm… is it in harmony – so full of peace?
Or contentment – with, we all are at ease.

Rhythm… is it when a friend whispers?
Or in the falling tears.

Rhythm… is it in bird's chirping?
Or in a frog's croaking.

Rhythm… is it a melody? – so pleasant to hear…
Or eternally vibrant, forever & ever!

BEING SHE

Neither did she hide her face,
Nor did she erase her trace.
But is terrified about,
life's forthcoming race!

Alas! another "Nirbhaya".

Like the sun, she wanted to shine,
with all the desires of a beautiful mind,
She started her hours with endless delight,
Beautiful heart, dreamed of a beautiful life.
Her journey from school to college,
...has come to an end
Happiness sprung.
A new life began.

A life with thousand reasons to smile,
with happiness all around, happy family she had.
Mother often said, she was as pretty as an angel.
And for Dad, she was, his adorable princess.
To further her ambition,
Entered in the corporate realm,
A well paid job. Talent revered.
Work appreciated. What else would she want!

On a fateful day...
"I will be late today", she said
Take care, worried words - mom uttered.
"Don't worry, Oh mother,
I am with my friends" she assured.
All pals in train, alighted, one by one,
She was just few stations away from home.
Alone, in the lonely compartment.

Never was she troubled,
by her loneliness or by the lonely realm.
Fearless was she,
didn't bother to look around.
Until the influx of a thunder broke,
...in a humanoid form.
A sudden blaze smacked,
pierced in a slot – were all "HE-s"
She was frightened to death,
Her heart pounded...
faster... faster than the...
moving high-speed train.
In a matter of few seconds,
her world turned upside down,
In the lusty, lecherous hands,
herself she found.
Beleaguered.....stripped!
Grabbed. Browbeaten. Subjugated.
She - Screamed. Screeched. Bawled.
Throbbing shrieks of hers,
evaded by the zipping train.
For being "SHE", all prices well paid!

left with...
Tattered clothe,
Shattered dreams,
Agonizing pain,
Grief-stricken body,
Dead soul!

And…
questions raised…
Or methodically blamed?
Who she?
Why late?
Why alone?
Wrong parenting?
Or Rebellious Offspring!
She seduced them?
Perhaps…
wrong attire…
triggered "HIS" desire.
Scandalous blames,
Endless questions,
Agony never ended, but began!

In the interim,
SHE was WHO?
--- a Valiant woman,
geared up to fight back.
Alas! to another "Nirbhaya"…
our Nation gives birth.

(dedicated to Nirbhaya & all the rape victims).

Honesty, in extreme,
an unwanted stream,
Bunged-up by plotters,
in today's corporate world!

Corporate World

They say, confidence she lacks and that she is weak, dim
and weedy,
She cries each day within, try hard to change herself and
her personalilty,
Is she not worth to survive in a corporate world? Is this
place not meant for her?
All play dirty politics, a game which is so filthy.
Here, each one tries to stomp on others, act smart, which
they aren't actually,
All try to move that prized piece of cheese, to have power
and authority.

This corporate world has become so ghastly!
No place left for humanity, no value for honesty.
Oh! This corporate world is so very ghastly!

They say, she is not born with that grey cell, which is
essential,
Essential is not honesty? Essential is not hard work and
talent?
What they require is some softy smooth butter with
foolish pieces of jests!
Is this what is left in this Corporate World?
Yet combating with the group, not losing her hope,
Worthy endeavors will one day be recognized, with it only
candor can swop.
This corporate world has become so ghastly!
No place left for humanity, no value for honesty.
Oh! This corporate world is so very ghastly!

Sometime, events shatter ordinary lives,
in many ways, due to various reasons.
Allow not yourself to be drowned,
in the melancholy blue ocean!

I am not yet shattered!

You cut my wings and demanded not to fly,
You pulled me back, insisted not to touch the sky,
You fastened my lips, forced me nothing to say,
You as well trapped me by jamming my way,
But to me all these never mattered…
Sorry to tell you… I am not yet shattered!

You stabbed my existence several times,
You killed my worth with your spites,
Only tears given to my meandered eyes,
Visions blurred, nothing there now lies,
But to me all these never mattered…
Sorry to tell you… I am not yet shattered!

Agonizing pain my soul has gone through,
Stranded was my life, yes… I was marred by you,
You forced me to exist in this world like vermin,
You slaughtered me with your malicious mien.
But to me all these never mattered…
Sorry to tell you… I am not yet shattered.

Shattered is my life
Shattered is my dream
Shattered is my soul
Shattered is my vision
Shattered are my ideas
Shattered are my whims
Shattered is my endurance
Shattered is my destiny
Yet, I say with glee
Shattered is not ME!
Shattered is not ME!

Dear Life,

Agreed,

Battles made me stronger, by each passing day,

but,

I need a break too!

Her Battle in the Corporate World

She fights, fights, and fights, every day for her rights,
Try hard each day not to lose her inner might.
Every day she encounters new challenges on her way,
It helps her become a stronger human, by each passing day.

Some foes, who can never think of any right,
Always stand on her way, looking at her way upright.
Tons of negativity passes through them,
Tries to destroy her esteem and occurrence.

They whack on her face with their cruel expressions,
They hurt her self esteem, with their spiteful words.
They look, stare and give a nasty gesture,
Kills her within destroying her quintessence?

Some think she is mad, some think, that she is dupe,
Some never consider her… inside the human loop!
She understand, very well, that life is not an easy journey,
But some filthy types, ends up driving her crazy.

No matter what she seeks, at the end of this battle,
Does it count, if the path ahead is unclear?
With courage she is her way to righteousness,
Of course, she wouldn't give up, until her last breath!

A worried man grumbled,
for being father of three daughters,
dim-witted was he,
to understand life's mystery.
His future was tremendously beautiful & bright,
wouldn't he will have three loving hearts,
and homes to welcome him upright!
------ daughters are for life!

A daughter

Flower's fragrance,
Sun's shine,
Moon's elegance,
Rose's petals,
Sea's waves,
Poet's beautiful poem,
An artist's art,
A rhythm,
Nightingale's melodious tune,
Rain's drizzle,
Night's silence,
Day's brightness,
Beautiful smile,
Harmony,
Serenity,
Faith,
Worship,
Nature's beauty,
A living miracle,

Marvelous creation of almighty,
... a daughter,

Why her occurrence do we slaughter?

--- revere her, love her and accept her.

How I wish,

Bosses to be teachers, good leaders, motivators…

not just…

an evil conspirators!

My Terrified Boss

Agreed...
I am stupendously talented,
Mind-blowingly good at work,
But, this shall not make you feel endangered.
I have no plans on you to attack,
Or to snatch your position & status,
believe me, I've got no interest!

Agreed...
I am immensely brilliant,
rather a Super Genius!
But, you are surely not my target.
My aim is beyond your unruliest thoughts.
Our visions are different & poles apart,
With you, I was never impressed!

Agreed,
I have got prodigious ideas,
which your grey cell deny to generate.
But, your disgraced plots and superfluous blames,
will not slay me or harm my poise,
No way, am going to get defamed!

Boss,
It's your life, your aim and your journey
You may aspire to spend rest of your life,
in this 4 by 4 cubicle. And for me,
I have got lot more to explore.
With consent, I say these words,
allow not your comfort zone,
… to become your comatose tomb!
All I wish is good luck!

PATRIOTIC

Salutation to UAE

Dear UAE,

Beautiful Land,
With Golden sands,
Kindhearted people,
And generous hands.

Hardwork you value,
You value sincerity,
Fairness you believe in,
That's your inner beauty.

We love you for what you are,
You are home for one,
You are home for all,
A nation truly to adore!

Let's say with pride and glee
We salute you UAE
Let's say with pride and glee
We salute you UAE

You have given vim,
to so many dreams,
for throbbing hearts,
you healed them within.
People from different realm,
find here a sweet home,
A nation full of vivacity,
We revere your generosity.

We respect you for what you are
You are home for one
You are home for all
A nation truly to adore

Let's say with pride and glee
We salute you UAE
Let's say with pride and glee
We salute you UAE

Ever Best India

Such grand and valuable treasure of traditions, my India holds.,
Neither does it equates to worldly gems nor gold's'.
It values human kind and it cradles human race,
being an "Indian", the whole world, I proudly face.
An epitome of wisdom, yet very modest,
with worldly knowledge, fulfills all quests
My beautiful country India,
Ever green, ever best!

SAD

Murdered was she,
by her inner agony,
through her own hands.

Only she knew,
what she was going through
inside.

With her own doubts, fears,
and terrors
she failed to combat !

her qualms,
of where her future lies,
… yearned to close her eyes

I yearn to close my eyes

My heart in a poignant state…
…every moment & hour,
No glimpse of good in anything,
My future stores nothing, I realized,
I yearn to close my eyes.

Barren ways, verve so infertile,
Blurred vision with zilch notion,
With self melee dismal I am,
Confined I am with deceipt, hatred and lies
I yearn to close my eyes.

Mystified & vague horizon,
Bleak & inept realism,
Or am I sightless to perceive the ray of hope,
Devastated within, if you know why?
I yearn to close my eyes

Set her free…

from the unnecessary norms of the society,

let her be… “be”!

No More I Desire

From Father to Daughter

Here you go with your verve, to hold you, no more I desire
Search for the ultimate aspire, to seize you, no more I desire

Take away the freedom you much loved, enjoy the sovereignty,
Enjoy each moment of this existence, take pleasure in life's journey
Cherish this era with the treasure of your spirit and will
Flow with the waves of life and have your dreams fulfill
To cleave you for the sake of this world, no more I desire.
Search for the ultimate aspire, to seize you, no more I desire

The treasure of your flair, will show you the way to victory
Self-belief with wits and will power will help you to succeed.
Let me free you from the customs and mores of this society

Here I give you wings to fly, enjoy the life with utmost liberty
To pull you back from your yearning, no more I desire
Search for the ultimate aspire, to seize you, no more I desire

There you go with your verve, to hold you, no more I desire
Search for the ultimate aspire, to seize you, no more I desire

We have the privilege to choose a friend…

Be vigilant, not are all godsent.

Complexes of Inferiority

I know you are dear friend of mine,
since a very long time.
But with you, I know, I will never be fine.
Although we are friends since childhood,
I want you to go away far-off from my life.
You pull me back from whatever I want to do,
I blame you for not achieving what I wanted to.
You make me believe that I am good for nothing
and that I will never succeed in life.
You think I am hideous
and have unpleasant qualities in rife.
Because of you, I doubted my self worth,
Love was lost, rise stopped
Creativity faded, thoughts dead,
Scared to dream. "Fears" all that I have!
Enough of you ruling.
Enough of me losing.
No chance to you any more,
Let me be, what I want to be,
Leave me and make me free
Go away....
Oh, complexes of inferiority...
With you, I don't want to be!

Sometimes,
the only comrade I have is...
my loneliness.

At times,
It gives peace,
at times, scares!

Alone

The world entire thought I am wrong,
I was still going strong.
With a hope that I have you beside me.

Drops of rain, blow of breeze…
did not embrace me either,
Yet I survived with a hope, that you will accept me,

Sparkles of stars and rays of sun…
did not endorse me,
Never did I bother, with a hope that, you will care for me,

Smile betrayed me,
Happiness left me alone,
Yet l endured with a hope that, you will be there for me,

Sadly,
in the hands of this deceitful world,
I am left Alone!

Broken hearts.
Shattered dreams.
Weeping eyes.
Period.
Life has lots more to offer.

Broken Heart

Broken heart of mine, wrecked into millionth of pieces,
each pieces of it whimpers and cries out of pain.
Beneath me lies the melancholy vim, destroys me deep within,
slaying my esteem and essence.
My heart rambles all around, in search of my self-worth;
my serenity is lost in the midst of driving rain.
I crave for the cloudless life I desired for,
blame who… for my lap is filled with stars of ill-omen.